THE GREAT RACE

The Great Race

by David Bouchard

Paintings by Zhong-Yang Huang

RAINCOAST BOOKS

Vancouver

Tonight,

as they had done many nights before, the old woman and her
granddaughter took out paper cutouts of the twelve that
had taken part in the Great Race.

The small girl spread them out carefully on her bed, and
her grandmother nodded in approval.

"Yes, child, there were eleven animals and a dragon — a mystical
dragon. And, yes, they were as you have shown them to be in your
cutouts. The loyal dog, the brave rooster, the fiery dragon, the
hardworking ox —" and here the old woman slowly bent and let her
aged fingers linger on the cutout of the ox "— the secretive snake, the
obstinate horse, the reliable pig, the fortunate rabbit, the cautious
goat, the vain monkey, the restless tiger, and the cunning rat."

The old woman looked at her granddaughter. "You have done a
wonderful thing with your paper, child, only you have placed the
animals in the wrong order. You must listen more carefully to
understand where each one was placed. Remember, it is not who won
that matters. It is the order in which they placed that is most
important. Listen carefully so that you can come to understand why
each animal placed where it did. And, no, the story has
not changed since I told it to you last."

Long ago,

when the moon was young and her influence was held in highest regard by all people, the Great Buddha summoned the dragon and eleven animals to meet with him.

They met on a rocky hill that looked out over a desert. Beyond the desert was a forest thick with trees. Beyond the forest was a range of mountains whose peaks were covered with snow. And beyond the mountains was a vast sea that stretched as far as the eye could see. On the other side of the sea lay the Jade City, the city of perpetual caring, peace, and never-ending opportunity for all people.

The Great Buddha sat on a rock in front of the twelve and said, "I have gathered you here to run a race to the Jade City. One of you will come first — not the greatest, but first. One of you will come last — not the weakest, but twelfth. You will end up stretched out like beads on a necklace, and this will determine the order of your appearance for all matters of earthly importance. You must cross the desert, then the forest, then the mountains, and finally the sea. When I leave, you can begin."

Having said this, the Great Buddha rose to his feet. A dust storm grew around him, forcing the animals to shut their eyes tight. When the dust-filled heavens cleared, all but two of the twelve had disappeared. The race had begun.

The pig and the dog, who were good friends, were left alone on the hill. Eventually they made their way down, but their progress was slow, for the pig's stoutness made him wobble. Occasionally the dog, who could have easily been much farther ahead, would take a little run forward. Then, looking back and seeing that the pig had hardly moved, he would return.

"What is wrong, pig? We must hurry if we are to catch up with the others."

"I cannot go faster," said the pig as he plopped down, breathless.

"But we must. You know the significance of this race. If you do not try harder, you will be placed last."

Hearing this, the pig sighed and used all his strength to pull up his swollen body, only to fall back with a loud thud. "It is no use. The sun is hot and I am too tired. I will go faster when it is dark and cooler. But you go on."

The dog cast a worried look at his friend. "But you will die out here by yourself. I cannot let that happen. I will stay with you."

With another great effort, the pig heaved himself up and gently scratched behind the dog's ear with a careful hoof. "This is too kind of you. Staying with me will also cost you a favorable position. You will surely be placed no better than eleventh."

"Perhaps, but you are my friend," said the dog. "We will travel as slowly as you like for however long it takes. My only concern is how we will eat and drink."

The pig then gazed at the dog fondly. "Ah, my friend, there I can help. I know how to find things beneath the ground. Fear not. I will make sure we have enough to eat and water to slake our parched throats."

And so it was that the race began with the pig and the dog all but out of the running and with only ten left to place.

Three days passed. By this time the remaining animals had neared the edge of the desert and could feel the cool of the forest. The proud dragon, with the cocky rooster close beside him, had pulled ahead.

In a cloud of fire and with a beating of wings, they entered a small village at the desert's edge, appearing in the yard of a farmer who was quite startled by the dragon's seeming ferocity.

"I must have water!" roared the dragon. "And I must have it now."

"Yes!" crowed the rooster. "Bring us water, for if you do not, my friend will turn you into a cinder."

Hastily the farmer showed them to the well, where the dragon quickly emptied six buckets of water and loudly called for more. Just then, as the rooster tried hard to catch the drops of water falling from the dragon's mouth, he heard a frenzied commotion behind the farmhouse. It was a familiar sound!

He rounded the corner to the sight of wings, feathers,
dust, and panicky chickens scattered everywhere. It took little time to
locate a fox crouched low next to an overturned barrel.

Quicker than the wink of an eye or a squirrel up a tree, the rooster
screamed and flew headlong at the fox. Surprised and frightened, the
fox tucked his tail between his legs and scurried back into the desert.

Victory! The puffed-up rooster turned to the chickens
that now lined the top of the fence.

"Good evening, ladies," he said. "Your home is lush and yet near the
desert. I find this most appealing as I have always
had a passion for the sun."

"Why, thank you, courageous sir," answered a plump pullet. "Yes, we
do have an abundance of sun, but we have no husband." She simpered
and fluffed out her feathers. "As you have seen, there are desert foxes
lurking near. A husband would have to be extremely
brave to live here with us."

The rooster puffed himself up even more. He crowed and beat his
wings. "I have no fear of foxes and would be honored to
watch over you while waiting for the sun to rise."

So it was that the rooster stayed on the farm, sealing his place as
tenth for all matters of future importance.

Back at the well, the dragon, his thirst quenched, rose slowly into the air and flew over the forest toward the mountains, while on the far side of the same village, the monkey and the goat had arrived at a small, clear pond surrounded by lush grass.

The goat paced up and down the small patch of grass, nervously looking for the dangers that might lie ahead. He turned and hurried back to the monkey, who was staring at his own reflection in the water.

"Good heavens, goat," the monkey murmured, "will you stop your fretting. There is nothing out there that will harm you." This the monkey said without once lifting his eyes from the water into which he was staring. "Come here please and look at this." His dark eyes in the reflection were soft yet bright, his fur thick, his mouth protruding and firm.

"I have never looked as good as I do in this pond," the monkey said. "Do you not agree?" He had spoken without even looking at the goat. He could not tear his eyes away from his reflection. "I will never leave this place," he added.

The timid goat turned toward the village and said, "And I believe I will stay here with you." He bent his two front knees and lay down, tucking himself up next to the monkey. "I dread all the attention that comes with this race. Furthermore, we have here the three necessities of life — food, warmth, and a place to call home. The Great Buddha can place me where he will. I am happy to have been chosen as one of the twelve."

And so it was that the third day came to an end with the monkey finishing ninth, the goat eighth, and only seven left to place.

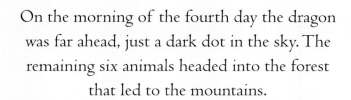

On the morning of the fourth day the dragon was far ahead, just a dark dot in the sky. The remaining six animals headed into the forest that led to the mountains.

The snake had slowly insinuated himself into the horse's affections and now lay wrapped around his neck. "Let me be your eyes as the forest thickens and darkens," he hissed. "Run like the wind, and together we will reach the mountains well ahead of the others."

And the horse did run hard, galloping with a thundering noise. But when they came to a fork in the road and the horse veered off to the left, the snake spit and lifted his head as if to bite. "No! This is the wrong path! You must listen to me or let me down! I will make my own way, foolish horse!"

"Nay, you will not!" the horse replied, running hard. "You have made good use of my speed. Now I need you to guide me through the trees."

And no matter what the angry snake said, the stubborn horse did not listen. Nor did he stop, but galloped on until night descended and they had become lost forever in the deep woods.

This was how the horse came to be placed seventh and the snake sixth.

After three more days, the tiger, the rabbit, the ox, and the rat found themselves in the cold and snowy mountains. Of the dragon nothing could be seen, for the wind whipped snow into their faces and made them shiver as if one.

"I ca-cannot go on," chattered the rabbit, the clacking of his teeth loud even in the roar of the wind.

"Then stay," growled the impatient tiger. "Your legendary luck will not help you up here. You will soon freeze."

"Hop on my back," offered the ox. "We have not far to go and I can carry you the rest of the way."

"Me, too!" cried the rat as he shot up the thick leg of the powerful ox.

"Weaklings," muttered the tiger, forging ahead in an attempt to see through the snow, all the while wondering what had become of the dragon.

Soon the snow ceased to fall
and the wind became less fierce. Then,
with mounting excitement, the four
animals began to descend. And when
three more days had passed, they came out
of the mountains and into a big meadow
where they could smell the salt tang of the
sea. Yet all the tiger could think of was
that the dragon had now been gone for a
very long time. Where could he be?

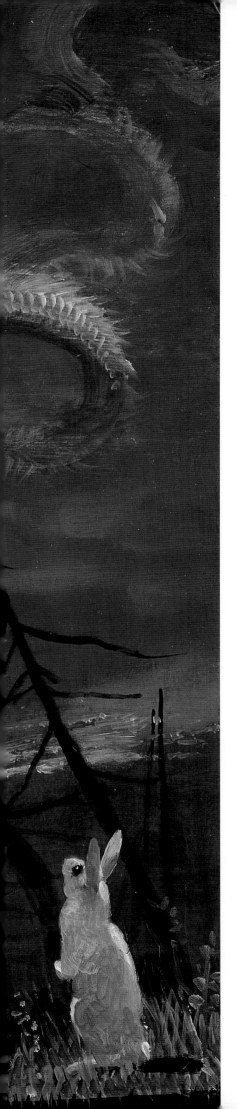

That afternoon, as the four trudged through the high grass of the meadow, a spectacular flame shot down from the sky, scorching the path in front of them. The four travelers stopped in their tracks.

His wings beating in the air, the dragon bellowed, "I have been to the gates of the Jade City. I have seen the masses of people waiting in blind admiration for the winners to arrive. I know that glory awaits the one who arrives first.

"But there are eight wolves, their teeth red with blood, who wait on either side of the gates for the contestants to arrive. I take it upon myself to lead them into the heavens where my friend the Great Bear will keep them under constant guard. Let these wolves sit for all time in the open sky and let them look upon us from a distance and from a place where we will always be able to see their eyes shining bright in the darkness."

His message ended, the dragon rose into the air and quickly flew over the sea in the direction from which he had come.

A few hours later the four animals reached the sea. It stretched before them in the late-afternoon sun, a vast expanse of water that seemed limitless.

The tiger's eyes flashed as he paced restlessly back and forth. "The dragon is right," he purred. "Fame and power do await me when I enter the Jade City first."

The rabbit leaped in a quick bound up onto a rock. "Do not underestimate my speed," he said in a careful voice, the cold and despair of the mountains not entirely forgotten. "I know that you are not fond of water, tiger. Perhaps we can together negotiate the order in which we will finish, and then seek a more pleasant way to the city."

"You are also afraid of water, rabbit," the tiger said with some disgust. "Do not try to fool me." He continued to pace among the rocks. "Nonetheless, I do like the idea of finding a safer road than the sea."

Sensing the anxiety of his traveling mates, the clever rat ran up a leg of the ox and onto his back. "Before we ponder too long over who should finish where, it might be wise to learn just how wide the sea actually is. If I were to stand up here on your back, ox, and you were to swim out a way, I could see how far we would have to swim. Then we might better judge to whom the advantage belongs."

The animals all agreed that this seemed a good plan.

And so the ox, with the rat high on his back, swam out to sea.

The ox swam for two days. The sea was cold and dark gray, and the water heaved up in immense waves. Alone on that sea, the ox with the rat on his back was no more than a speck.

"Rat, do you see nothing yet?" he asked repeatedly.

The answer was always the same. "I see no land, but I see birds on the horizon. Do not stop now."

On the morning of the twelfth day since the beginning of the race, the rat spotted the land they had been so desperately seeking.

"It is no use," the crafty rat said to the ox. "We will never find land. We will have to seek some other way to the Jade City. Let us return to our friends, who must be worrying about us."

Obeying the rat, the ox turned and swam back. As he did so, the rat slipped unnoticed into the dark, rough water and swam to the shore that led to the Jade City.

It was not until much later that the ox realized he was alone. In his grief he cried out, "Rat! I have been careless. You have fallen from my back. Do not be afraid. I will find you."

With these words he turned and swam until he, too, reached the shore of the Jade City. Then, more tired than he had ever been before, he began walking toward the gates of the city where he hoped to find someone who could help him search for the rat.

"Well," said the old woman as she arched her back, "the tiger and the rabbit did in the end take the long way around. They passed through a hundred kingdoms and suffered many hardships, but the luck of the rabbit prevailed. Exhausted, their fur matted, they reached the Jade City at last, finishing third and fourth.

"And it was much later before the dragon finally returned. He entered the city on a night that was as black as coal, and the bright eyes of eight wolves could be seen flickering in the sky, staring down at the one destined to place fifth."

The old woman looked at her granddaughter and smiled. "Not much is said of what happened after the race, child. What is known for certain, however —" and here she gently picked up the cutout of the ox "— is that a weary ox entered the Jade City with only the welfare of a small rat on his mind. And in so doing he sealed his fate for all time as the second of the twelve animals in the zodiac. Now, child, shall we begin again?"

The Chinese Zodiac

More than five thousand years ago the people of China began to think of themselves and their life paths in terms of the passage of time rather than the placement of the stars. The exact moment in time that a person is born is seen as a reflection of what that person will be and what fortune he or she will encounter throughout the course of a lifetime. One full cycle is sixty years, which is further divided into five twelve-year rotations.

Each year is associated with one of twelve animals. Exactly who determined which twelve animals would be used is a mystery. This book tells just one of many stories of how they came to place in the order that we know them.

Traditionally the year someone is born governs his or her personality, and a person shares characteristics with the animal that is associated with that year. The year before and after your birth, and the animals for those years, also influence your personality, but to a lesser degree. See if you can find your year of birth and animal in the list that follows.

Rat

1996, 1984, 1972, 1960, 1948, 1936, 1924, 1912, 1900

You are likely to be a collector, a gatherer of "stuff." You are proud and popular and are not afraid of hard work. You are quite sociable and outgoing, although you should be careful not to be viewed as too opportunistic. After all, you are cunning and ambitious. Those who criticize you will say that you are too critical and something of a gossip. However, they won't criticize you too openly because they will know that you might bite.

Ox

1997, 1985, 1973, 1961, 1949, 1937, 1925, 1913, 1901

None can work as hard as you because you are methodical, patient, and always dependable. You are the loyal one in whom many will put their trust. And yet, in spite of all this, you will want to watch your stubborn streak and the perception that you are inflexible, single-minded, and someone who holds a grudge. You may be slow when it comes to accomplishing things, but you always come through eventually.

Tiger

1998, 1986, 1974, 1962, 1950, 1938, 1926, 1914, 1902

Although you are unpredictable, you don't mind being called passionate or impulsive because you love being the center of attention. Furthermore, you have a great sense of humor. Your courage makes you a natural-born leader. However, your brashness and occasional irritability can prove unattractive to other people, so be careful.

Rabbit

1999, 1987, 1975, 1963, 1951, 1939, 1927, 1915, 1903

You are kind, gracious, and friendly. Everywhere you go you are popular and luck is something you have in abundance. However, your good fortune does not make other people envious because you are always modest and generous. Nevertheless, you do have a tendency to be shy and sentimental, and from time to time you engage in bouts of self-indulgence.

Dragon

2000, 1988, 1976, 1964, 1952,
1940, 1928, 1916, 1904

It must be awfully difficult for you not to appear overconfident, knowing you have so much strength, energy, and depth. An extrovert like you must work at not appearing brash and unreasonable. Of course, your charisma and deliciously positive attitude go a long way when it comes to making friends. Often given to dramatics and possessed of a vivid imagination, you can also be moody and something of a perfectionist.

Snake

2001, 1989, 1977, 1965, 1953,
1941, 1929, 1917, 1905

As the philosopher of the twelve animals, your talent, wisdom, grace, and intuition are among your best qualities. But you can also be secretive, stingy, and a bit vain. Your financial good fortune will allow you to achieve the luxuries you always seem to crave. And if you use your good qualities to help others, you will be truly fortunate and always find the right path.

Horse

2002, 1990, 1978, 1966, 1954,
1942, 1930, 1918, 1906

You have a tendency not to finish projects that you start, and patience is something difficult for you to master. However, your boundless energy, confidence, and optimism help you to make friends easily, even if your obstinate streak can be worrisome at times. A free spirit, you like to travel by yourself, and your nonconformity means you really don't care what other people think.

Goat

2003, 1991, 1979, 1967, 1955,
1943, 1931, 1919, 1907

Being mild-mannered, cautious, and shy doesn't necessarily mean you are weak. These traits are often associated with gentleness and creativity, and rightfully so, for that is what you are. Unfortunately your kindness and generosity are sometimes overshadowed by your pessimistic and withdrawn nature, but don't dwell on such things. You worry enough already.

Monkey

2004, 1992, 1980, 1968, 1956,
1944, 1932, 1920, 1908

You are very smart, and you know it. Vanity can sometimes be your downfall. Still, you are curious, generally happy, and energetic. To you, life is a barrel of laughs. Watch out for that superiority complex, though, and try not to get ahead of yourself.

Rooster

2005, 1993, 1981, 1969, 1957,
1945, 1933, 1921, 1909

Bravery is one of your best features, even if you can be a bit reckless sometimes. Usually, though, you are disciplined and reliable. Perhaps the most misunderstood of the twelve animals, sometimes due to a lack of tact and a touch of conceit, you are nevertheless pleasantly witty and fun to be with.

Dog

2006, 1994, 1982, 1970, 1958, 1946,
1934, 1922, 1910

Intelligent, honest, affectionate, and loyal, you are the ultimate friend and probably the most likable of the twelve animals. Something of a worrywart, you often have a hard time finding the silver lining in a black cloud. Nevertheless, you are a team player and quite selfless.

Pig

2007, 1995, 1983, 1971, 1959,
1947, 1935, 1923, 1911

You put your heart and soul into your work and are known for being loyal and utterly reliable. None are as generous and self-sacrificing as you, and frankly, you have to learn how to say no or you may find yourself getting into too much trouble. Of course, when you do get into trouble, you will always be the one to bear the blame.

For Kim

– D.B.

To the memory of my grandmother

– Z.Y.H.

First published in Canada in 1997 by

Raincoast Books
8680 Cambie Street
Vancouver, B.C. v6p 6m9
(604) 323-7100

3   5   7   9   10   8   6   4   2

CANADIAN CATALOGUING IN PUBLICATION DATA

Bouchard, Dave, 1952-
The great race

ISBN 1-55192-090-5

I. Huang, Zhong-Yang, 1949- II. Title.
PS8553.O759G73 1997   jC813'.54   C97-910158-1
PZ7.B6589Gr 1997

Designed by Dean Allen
Project Editor: Michael Carroll
Copy Editor: Bruce Serafin

Printed in Hong Kong

*Raincoast Books gratefully acknowledges the support of the Canada Council, the Department
of Canadian Heritage, and the British Columbia Arts Council.*